LiKE PLANTS!

PLANTS GROW!

Mary Dodson Wade

Series Science Consultant:
Mary Poulson, PhD
Associate Professor of Plant Biology
Department of Biological Sciences
Central Washington University
Ellensburg, WA

Series Literacy Consultant:
Allan A. De Fina, PhD
Dean, College of Education/Professor of Literacy Education
New Jersey City University
Past President of the New Jersey Reading Association

CONTENTS

WORDS TO KNOW

pollen (PAH lihn)—A dust-like powder that flowers make. Pollen is needed to make seeds.

tough (TUF)—Strong, and hard to break.

PARTS OF A PLANT

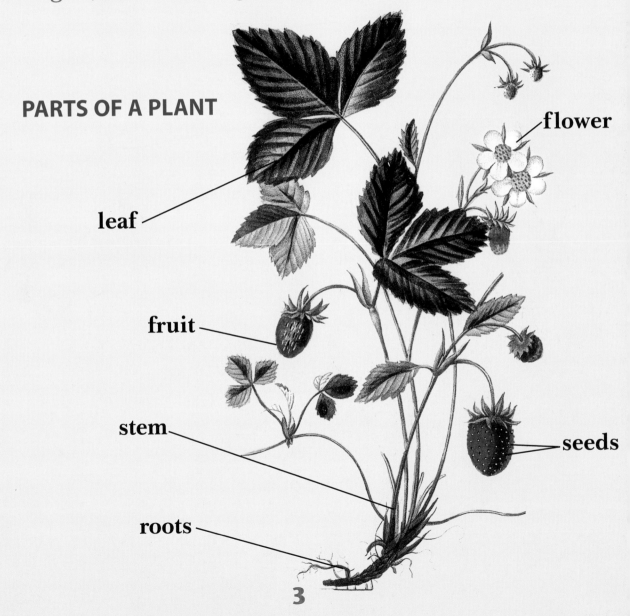

leaf

flower

fruit

stem

seeds

roots

3

Apple seeds have a tough cover.

seed

START WITH SEEDS

Most plants grow from seeds. A new plant is inside the seed. Seeds have a **tough** cover. Seeds soak up water to make the cover soft. The plant inside the seed starts to grow.

pea seeds

This pea seed is starting to grow a root.

root

ROOTS
START TO GROW

A small root comes out of the seed. It grows down into the soil. The root brings water from the soil to the plant. Roots hold a plant in one place.

A tree's big roots hold it in place.

STEMS
HAVE MANY JOBS

The stem starts to grow, too. It grows out of the ground. The stem carries water to the leaves. It also carries food to the roots. Stems hold a plant up.

Some plants have many stems, like this shrub.

stem

A pea plant's leaves capture the sun's energy.

LEAVES
MAKE FOOD

Leaves grow out of the stem.
Green leaves take in sunlight.
The leaves use air,
water, and the
sunlight to make
food for the plant.
The plant uses the
food to grow.

FLOWERS
BLOOM

Many plants have flowers. The flowers often have bright colors. Insects, birds, and other animals come to the bright flowers. Their bodies pick up **pollen**. They carry the pollen to other flowers.

This pea plant has flowers.

This pea flower is turning into a fruit

FROM FLOWER TO
FRUIT

The tiny pollen grains go deep inside the flower. Then the flower turns into a fruit. A fruit has seeds inside it. Why do plants make fruit? To spread the seeds to new places!

These green peas are the fruit of the pea plant.

BACK TO
SEEDS

Wind can blow the fruit and its seeds. Animals eat fruit and then leave the seeds behind. If the fruit floats, water can carry the seeds far away. New plants grow from these seeds. The life cycle starts all over again.

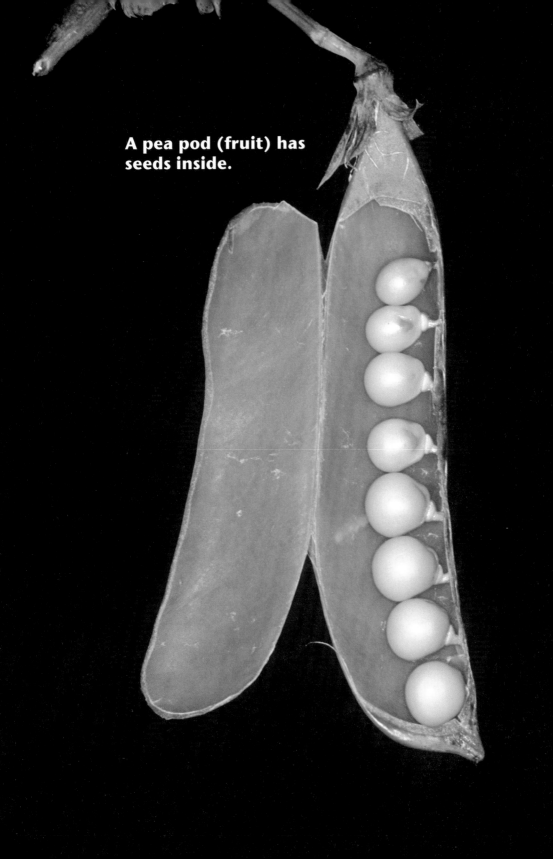

A pea pod (fruit) has
seeds inside.

LIFE CYCLE OF A
PLANT

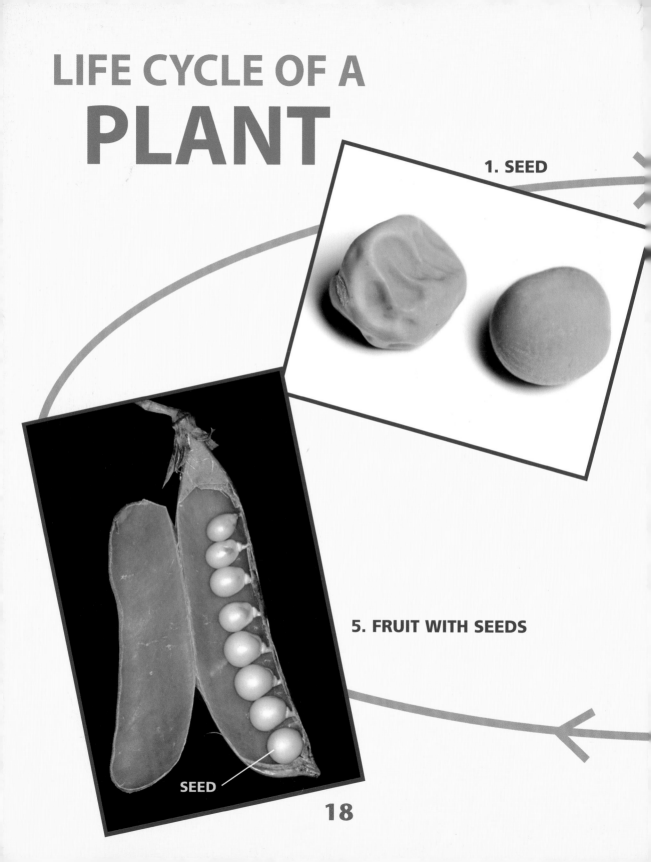

1. SEED

5. FRUIT WITH SEEDS

SEED

18

2. SPROUTING SEED

LEAVES

STEM

ROOTS

3. SEEDLING

4. PLANT WITH FLOWERS

19

CAN YOU SEE PART OF A PLANT'S LIFE CYCLE?

You will need:
* bean seeds
* paper towel
* water
* plate

1. Wet a paper towel and fold it in half.

2. Place the wet towel on a plate on your kitchen counter.

3. Place a few bean seeds in the fold of the paper towel.

4. Make sure the towel does not dry out. Wet the towel again when needed.

5. What happens to the seeds after a day? After two days? After three days?

6. Do you see anything growing from the seeds?

LEARN MORE

BOOKS

Bodach, Vijaya Khisty. *Seeds*. Mankato, Minn.: Capstone Press, 2007.

Stone, Lynn M., and Ray James. *Plant Cycle*. Vero Beach, Fla.: Rourke Publishing, 2007.

Tagliaferro, Linda. *The Life Cycle of a Sunflower*. Mankato, Minn.: Capstone Press, 2007.

LEARN MORE

WEB SITES

"A Walk in the Forest."

<http://www.urbanext.uiuc.edu/woods>

University of Illinois. The Great Plant Escape.

<http://www.urbanext.uiuc.edu/gpe>

U.S. Department of Agriculture. Sci4Kids. "Plants."

<http://www.ars.usda.gov/is/kids/plants/plantsintro.
htm>

INDEX

Enslow Elementary, an imprint of Enslow Publishers, Inc.
Enslow Elementary® is a registered trademark of
Enslow Publishers, Inc.

Library of Congress Cataloging-in-Publication Data

Wade, Mary Dodson.
   Wade, Mary Dodson.
      Plants grow! / Mary Dodson Wade.
   p. cm. — (I like plants!)
   Summary: "Information about the life cycle and parts of a
plant for young readers"—Provided by publisher.
   Includes bibliographical references and index.
   ISBN-13: 978-0-7660-3152-4 (library ed.)
   ISBN-10: 0-7660-3152-7 (library ed.)
   1. Growth (Plants)—Juvenile literature. I. Title.
   QK731.W32 2009
   571.8'2—dc22

                  2007039453

ISBN-13: 978-0-7660-3612-3 (paperback)
ISBN-10: 0-7660-3612-X (paperback)

Printed in the United States of America

10 9 8 7 6 5 4 3 2 1

Note to Parents and Teachers: The *I Like Plants!* series supports the
National Science Education Standards for K–4 science. The Words to
Know section introduces subject-specific vocabulary words, including
pronunciation and definitions. Early readers may need help with
these new words.

Photo Credits: © Alina Solovyova-Vincent/iStockphoto.com, p. 20;
BSIP/Photo Researchers, Inc., p. 3; Clive Schaupmeyer/
AGStockUSA/Photo Researchers, Inc., p. 15; © Dr. James
Richardson/Visuals Unlimited, pp. 17, 18 (fruit); Enslow Publishers,
Inc., pp. 13, 19 (plant with flowers); Jane Katirgis/Enslow
Publishers, Inc., p. 10; © Malcolm Romain/iStockphoto.com, 19
(seedling); Martin Shields/Photo Researchers, Inc., pp. 5, 18 (seed);
© Michael Durham/Minden Pictures, p. 12; © Nigel Cattlin/Visuals
Unlimited, pp. 6, 9, 19 (sprouting seed); Shutterstock, pp. 4, 7, 8,
11, 16; © Tony Evans/npl/Minden Pictures, p. 2; © Wally
Eberhart/Visuals Unlimited, pp. 1, 14, 22.

Cover Photo: © Mark Moffett/Minden Pictures

Enslow Elementary
an imprint of
Enslow Publishers, Inc.
40 Industrial Road
Box 398
Berkeley Heights, NJ 07922
USA
http://www.enslow.com